ALMOST TRAGIC: SHAKESPEARE'S NOT-DEAD HEROINES
by Laura Neill

Uproar Theatrics

LICENSING & PRODUCTION INQUIRIES
Uproar Theatrics, LLC.
hello@uproartheatrics.com I www.UproarTheatrics.com

Table of Contents

Note: These four short plays may be performed separately or as one full evening of theatre. If the plays are performed as a collection, the optional final scene brings characters from different plays together in a grand finale.

For more information, please visit UproarTheatrics.com

Cast breakdown
11-20F, 0-9M, flexible ensemble (minimum cast of 9 with doubling)

JULIET, a teenager. Her new husband just killed himself and she, um, didn't. Principal.

ROSALINE, a teenager. Half-heartedly playing the hero. Okay, quarter-heartedly. Principal.

WILLOW, a teenager. The apothecary's apprentice. Determined to get rid of the evidence. Principal.

ROMEO, a teenager. Killed himself with poison. Or did he mess it up? Supporting.

VERITY, a witch. An idealist. Wants to make a positive difference in the world. Principal.

LENNY, a witch. An anarchist. Wants to be entertained. Principal.

ELMGARD, a witch. A purist. Wants to follow the right path. Principal.

ABBY, principal, the daughter of Emilia and Iago.

BRITTANY, principal, Desdemona's cousin.

GERTRUDE Principal. Queen of Denmark. Really, really tired of dealing with all these men.

HAMLET Supporting. Prince of Denmark. So ready to be dead, and confused when he's not.

HORATIO Supporting. Hamlet's buddy.

LAERTES Supporting. Ophelia's brother. Originally planned to kill Hamlet but then felt bad about it and now he's alive and confused.

OSRIC Supporting. Court dude.

COURTIER 1 Supporting. A courtier in the court of Denmark. Has a couple lines. *Can double as Warrior Maidservant 1.

COURTIER 2 Supporting. A courtier in the court of Denmark. Has a couple lines.

COURTIERS Supporting. Non-speaking ensemble, as many as you'd like.

FORTINBRAS Supporting. Crown Prince of Norway. Really psyched about becoming King of Denmark.

AMBASSADOR Supporting. Fortinbras' ambassador to Denmark. Holds Fortinbras' hand through political stuff.

OPHELIA Principal. Not dead and ready to take revenge on Hamlet for killing her dad. *Can double as Fortinbras or Ambassador.

WARRIOR MAIDSERVANT 1 Supporting. One of Ophelia's entourage. Has a couple lines. *Can double as Courtier 1.

WARRIOR MAIDSERVANTS Supporting. Ophelia's entourage. Only speak to cheer for her. As many as you'd like.

CLAUDIUS Supporting, or a prop. Claudius is the one person in this play who's actually dead. You just need a body. Option to have someone playing the body twitch and moan until Gertrude's "thankfully, he's really dead."

A note on casting
All roles can be played by female or non-binary actors, regardless of the character's gender. If casting with additional genders, the following roles can be played by male actors: Verity and Elmgard in *After Hereafter*, and all speaking roles excluding Gertrude and Ophelia in *The Revenge of Gertrude.*

If you'd like to do the whole show with the minimum cast of 9, that means all of your characters from *Juliet Wakes Up*, *After Hereafter*, and *Iago's Daughter* will perform second (and in some cases, also third) roles in *The Revenge of Gertrude*.

Here's one way to make that happen – but feel free to switch the doubling and tripling around to match your company's needs:

Gertrude - doubled with Abby
Ophelia - doubled with Fortinbras, Brittany
Hamlet - doubled with Willow
Horatio - doubled with Verity
Laertes - doubled with Elmgard
Ambassador - doubled with Romeo
Osric - doubled with Lenny
Courtier 1 - doubled with Warrior Maidservant 1, Rosaline
Courtier 2 - doubled with Juliet, part of Warrior Maidservant ensemble

In this version, Claudius' body is a prop rather than a person, and Courtiers 1 and 2 become the Warrior Maidservants. You'll notice that Abby and Brittany are not in the optional final scene, allowing them to act as Gertrude and Ophelia there.

If you'd like to do the largest version of the play possible, then undouble everything, have 20+ ensembles of Courtiers and Warrior Maidservants, and make Claudius a person who dies very loudly until Gertrude's line "thankfully, he's really dead." This will yield you a cast of 60+.

Location for each piece
Juliet Wakes Up: Verona, Italy
After Hereafter: A drippy cave in Birnam Wood
Iago's Daughter: The chores alley of a nunnery
The Revenge of Gertrude: The court of Denmark
Optional final scene: A drippy cave in Birnam Wood; aboard a ship

Notes on intermission placement
An intermission is optional. If you'd like an intermission, I suggest placing it either after *After Hereafter* (to split the four plays in half) or after *Iago's Daughter* (if you're going to do the final scene and ham up the swordfight in Gertrude, to split the timing in half).

Content Modification
In *Juliet Wakes Up,* you can skip sexual allusions by cutting the lines between Willow's "You met him three days ago??" and Willow's "Can we clean up the evidence and get out of here??" so that the script reads: WILLOW: "You met him three days ago?? Whatever. Can we clean up the evidence and get out of here??"

Alternately, if you wish to just replace Juliet's line "And also the sex wasn't that good," you may use the replacement line "And also the night-time part wasn't that good."

No additional permission from Uproar Theatrics needed for either/both of these modifications.

A note about the optional final scene

The five-minute optional final scene is, well, optional! You have three choices:

1. If you'd like to have characters from three of the four shows cross paths in a grand finale, then this final scene is here for you.
2. If you'd prefer to simply do the four plays without the last scene, that is completely fine.
3. If you'd like to have the cast and crew individually or collectively write their OWN version of the final scene–anything from a sequel to one of the plays, to having characters from all four plays cross paths– you may!

If you'd like to write your own final scene, please clearly credit the playwright(s) in your program for that final scene, while making clear that the first four plays are by Laura Neill. You may write your version of the final scene on your own without Laura's guidance, if you like. OR, you may reach out to us to schedule a writing workshop with Laura's guidance. Our playwright will lead you through the process of writing a play by sharing possible ways of crafting characters and arcs, helpful tips for getting through writer's block, and in-the-moment feedback on your ideas during the workshop. This 90-minute workshop can be selected as a supplemental option when submitting your license request, or added after by emailing hello@uproartheatrics.com.

JULIET WAKES UP

A tomb. Not a lot onstage. Cold and darkness.

In stumbles JULIET, in a wedding dress, covered in blood.

JULIET

'Sblood 'sblood 'sblood!!!

ROSALINE

Blood!!

JULIET shrieks. She totally did not know Rosaline was there.

JULIET

Ghost! Vampire! Murderer!

ROSALINE

Um pretty sure you're the murderer, you're the one with blood all over your hands.

JULIET

I'm not—I just—he's DEAD.

ROSALINE

Yeah, he was dead before I got here, but like there was a vial or whatever, he poisoned himself, so like why do you have--

JULIET

He's dead. He's dead he's dead he's dead and I freaked out and took his dagger but then like I couldn't do it, I couldn't kill myself but it felt like I had to do SOMETHING like I had the dagger so I just well I freaked out and tried to put it back but I guess I missed because it sort of went in.

ROSALINE

You stabbed his dead body?

JULIET

I didn't MEAN TO, I was going to send myself to my eternal rest with my husband but then like--

ROSALINE

You stabbed his dead body.

JULIET

You're giving a lot of judgment for like a ghost or whatever.

ROSALINE

I'm not a GHOST. What the eff Juliet. Do you really not recognize me.

JULIET

Ummmm...

ROSALINE

It's ROSALINE! Your COUSIN! You could at least like remember that I exist! Not that anyone else does.

JULIET

Oh right. Sorry. Why?

ROSALINE

Why do I exist??

JULIET

Why are you like—here--

ROSALINE

Well back when your dead boyfriend was MY boyfriend the
friar came up with this whole stupid "pretend you're dead"
plot and I was like "NO THAT'S INSANE who would do
something that stupid" but then I remembered that you're
stupid and Romeo is REALLY STUPID so out of like family
loyalty or whatever I came to, like, save you.

JULIET

But you didn't save him.

ROSALINE

Like I said, dead when I got here. He killed himself, like,
really fast. There's also, like, another dead guy out there, but
maybe that was unrelated?

JULIET

But you weren't trying to save me--

ROSALINE

Girl I SHOOK you, you were really under.

JULIET

Okay but you could have at least hung out near my body or
like--

ROSALINE

It's been like FOUR HOURS, I had to pee--

JULIET

You let me almost kill myself because you had to pee??

ROSALINE

Girl you're the one who almost killed yourself! I am not
OBLIGATED to be here okay! I tried! Stop yelling at me!

                    JULIET

Stop yelling at ME!

                   ROSALINE

NO!

                    JULIET
SOMEONE IS GOING TO HEAR US!

                   ROSALINE
MAYBE YOU SHOULD HAVE THOUGHT OF THAT
BEFORE YOU STABBED A DEAD BODY!

                    JULIET
THEY'RE GOING TO THINK I KILLED HIM! AND THE
OTHER GUY! WHO'S THE OTHER GUY?

                   ROSALINE
YOUR OTHER FIANCE! LONDON! BUENOS AIRES!

                    JULIET

PARIS??

                   ROSALINE

SURE!

                    JULIET
I DON'T REALLY CARE BECAUSE HE WAS GROSS
BUT SOMEONE IS GOING TO HEAR US AND THINK I
KILLED THEM AND DRAG ME TO JAIL OR EXILE OR
WHATEVER!!

                    WILLOW

By'r rood SHUT UP.

            WILLOW emerges from the shadows of the

tomb.

ROSALINE and JULIET both scream.

ROSALINE and JULIET
Ghost!!

WILLOW
Yeah totally a ghost, I'm the Great Undead Ghost of Willow, I'm gonna haunt you forever if you don't shut up.

ROSALINE
Wait you don't look like a ghost.

WILLOW
No I totally am, I'm the all-powerful Ghost of Willow and I'm asking you to keep your voices down.

JULIET
I don't think ghosts are all-powerful.

ROSALINE
Yeah aren't they like condemned to wander the earth or whatever--

WILLOW
Whatever, maybe I'm just regular Willow, can you please shut up.

JULIET
I guess you said please that time--

WILLOW
And yet you're still talking.

JULIET

I'm allowed to express myself, okay, I just got married and
then my husband killed himself and then I accidentally
stabbed his dead body and apparently my gross fiance is also
dead, just like give me a second to feel feelings--

WILLOW

Where's the vial?

ROSALINE

The poison vial?

WILLOW

Yeah, a-duh.

JULIET

How do you know about the poison vial??

WILLOW

Because my stupid boss the stupid apothecary gave it to
stupid Romeo and if my stupid boss gets excommunicated or
whatever then I will too so I came to hide the stupid
evidence.

ROSALINE

Oh. Word.

JULIET

Don't call my husband stupid!

ROSALINE

Wasn't he though.

JULIET

Yes but that's not the point!

WILLOW

I literally do not care how you felt about your dead husband, I literally just need to cover up his death so if you could like--

JULIET

I don't know how I feel about my dead husband. Oh wow. I don't know how I feel. I feel sadness and anger and love but also--

WILLOW

Literally do not care--

JULIET

Oh wow I feel relief. I'm relieved. I'm the worst wife in the entire world but part of me is--

ROSALINE

Glad he's dead?

JULIET

How DARE you say such a thing—but yeah part of me is like actually glad because I am TOO YOUNG TO GET MARRIED to someone I met three days ago.

WILLOW

You met him three days ago???

JULIET

(And also the sex wasn't that good.)

> *JULIET gasps and puts her hands over her mouth.*

ROSALINE

That's the part that's a surprise to you?

JULIET

Like I wanted him to stay so we could go again because I
didn't, um, I heard there's supposed to be a good part and we
didn't get to that part, but he really just cared about his part
and then he like had to go, so--

WILLOW

Oh girl no. If any guy only cares about his part, you ditch
him. Okay?

ROSALINE

Or stab his dead body in a tomb. That works too.

WILLOW

Now can we clean up the evidence and get out of here??

JULIET

How are we supposed to CLEAN anything, I'm covered in
blood and like did you bring any cleaning supplies?

WILLOW

I didn't know there was going to be BLOOD, it's poison, I
mean--

ROSALINE

You are both so unprepared.

WILLOW

Um excuse me and your contribution is??

JULIET

You're sure he was dead, right.

WILLOW

What.

ROSALINE

Oh Paris was def dead like Romeo kind of went to town. Ooh and if Romeo like "disappears" people are gonna think he just murdered Paris and then ran so like that's actually a good plan we should just get rid of his body and then--

JULIET

But like Romeo like my husband like you're sure that the poison killed him right.

ROSALINE

For real?

JULIET

Like what if he wasn't, what if he wasn't, what if he wasn't and then I--

ROSALINE

Girl I CHECKED.

JULIET

But like how good did you check, did you--

ROSALINE

He was dead.

WILLOW

Are you sure. Because actually my problems personally would go away if this was like a stabby stabby murder and not a poison poison oops.

A noise from the other side of the tomb.

ROSALINE

What was that.

9

WILLOW
Um I don't know, like a rat.

JULIET
Does that mean the rats are like eating his body.

WILLOW
Probably.

ROSALINE
Shut up, she's traumatized!

WILLOW
Actually I think she killed him.

ROSALINE
No she didn't, don't try to make this a Capulet Montague thing okay.

JULIET
Hey shut up.

ROSALINE
He was definitely dead when I got here.

WILLOW
Well you're a Capulet too AND an ex so I'm not sure I believe you, maybe you both killed him.

JULIET
Hey--

ROSALINE
Well you're the one who gave him the poison so I'm pretty sure we're all like implicated at this point.

JULIET

HEY!!!

> *JULIET points toward the other side of the tomb.*
>
> *A bloody, almost-but-not-quite-dead ROMEO stumbles in.*
>
> *JULIET, ROSALINE, and WILLOW scream.*

ROSALINE

Holy rood he's not dead!

JULIET

He's not dead--

WILLOW

He's almost dead.

ROMEO

Help... me...

JULIET

Husband! Um!

ROSALINE

He's not going to make it.

JULIET

But he could—if we call for help--

ROSALINE

We can't call for help!

WILLOW

Who's going to help us??

ROSALINE

Who's going to believe us that we thought he was dead when he very clearly is not. And also we need everyone to think he murdered Paris and ran, like.

ROMEO

Help. Juliet--

WILLOW

And this tomb is in the middle of nowhere. The nearest apothecary is like sixteen miles away.

ROSALINE

He's not gonna make it no matter what we do.

ROMEO

Juliet—my love--

JULIET

I don't know what to do.

> *ROMEO was crawling toward JULIET but changes direction.*

ROMEO

Rosaline—I love you—you are my one true--

ROSALINE

Ew.

JULIET

He's dying, he doesn't mean it. He loves me.

12

ROMEO

I love you—just help me--

JULIET

What are we doing, we have to, we have to--

WILLOW

There's nothing to do.

JULIET

What do you mean there's NOTHING, we have to do
SOMETHING--

WILLOW

DO YOU WANT TO DIE TOO.

JULIET

NO. Obviously.

WILLOW

We're all on the Capulet side of this. If we show up
somewhere with a bloody Montague who let's face it is
gonna be dead by the time we get there, this isn't going to
end well.

ROSALINE

Girl I think you stabbed him kind of hard.

JULIET

I was just trying to get the thing back in the thing--

WILLOW

Were you?

ROMEO

Help—argh--

WILLOW

Unless you want to get prosecuted for his murder we're gonna need to hide the body. And for that to happen there has to be a body.

ROMEO collapses.

ROSALINE

Okay he's probably dead now.

JULIET

'Sblood--

WILLOW

No I don't think he's dead yet.

ROSALINE

You were the one who said he was almost dead.

WILLOW

Yeah but he's still breathing, I can see it.

JULIET

My husband--

ROSALINE

Girl you already stabbed him, clearly there was more to that story.

JULIET

I can't believe I had a husband.

WILLOW

Have. Almost had. Wait for it--

JULIET

I'm sorry my love--

> *And JULIET grabs the dagger sticking out of*
> *ROMEO and stabs him again. And maybe again.*
>
> *Until he is DEFINITELY dead.*

WILLOW

Right. So.

ROSALINE

Dead. Yup.

WILLOW

Yup.

JULIET
I killed him.

WILLOW

Yeah.

JULIET
I KILLED him.

ROSALINE

I mean so did I because honestly I could have gotten here
sooner, like I didn't rush over exactly as fast as I should
have. I mean it's not like he was ever there for me so like I
miiiight have sort of taken my time--

                    WILLOW
Ooh yeah, this is also your bad.

                    ROSALINE
Hey.

                    WILLOW
Okay yeah I guess I also killed him because I miiiiight have
mixed the poison a tiny bit stronger than I needed to.

                    ROSALINE
Oh by'r rood.

                    WILLOW
Like I'm new at this okay, who lets the apprentice mix the
actual poison, like I meant to make it less deadly but I think
I--

                    JULIET
I'm free.

              They quiet and look at her.

                    JULIET
I didn't mean to kill him, I know you don't believe me, but I
didn't, at least not on the surface, but also with the whole
death plan I can't say it didn't cross my mind like what the
flip am I doing, like why am I giving up my entire life and
my like princesshood and my mom for this guy who was in
love with someone else three days ago, am I really sure that
this is what I want, and then when I was taking the sleeping
potion thing like as I counted back from ten I got to eight
and I was like NO THIS ISN'T WHAT I WANT but then it
was too late and I was dead like fake dead right but also
when I realized that it also felt like I was dead dead like I
had gone from one totally controlled and patriarchal

16

relationship into another one into another one and I'm only
barely a person like what if I never got to actually be a
person because Romeo wasn't going to save me from the
thing, he was the thing, he was also the thing, and that's not
exactly his fault but also why didn't he care when I didn't
get to the part that felt good and why didn't he check in on
me more like why didn't he do any of the emotional labor in
our relationship and why didn't he even really TRY to ask
my parents for my hand in marriage like he just wanted to
cut me off my whole life because it was easier for him that
figuring it out with me, like isn't that such a man thing to do
like 'sblood like I really did think he was dead most of me
thought he was dead but also it felt kind of good to stab his
body.

> *ROSALINE grabs the dagger and stabs ROMEO
> too.*

WILLOW

Holy--

ROSALINE

He's already dead, I might as well get some catharsis too. He
didn't even answer my carrier pigeon when I thought I was
preggers.

WILLOW

By'r rood are you--

ROSALINE

Nah, I was just late, but he didn't know that and then
suddenly he was in love with someone else.

WILLOW

Wow you both really dodged a sword.

JULIET
Yeah. Sorry, Rosaline.

ROSALINE
Hey, if it wasn't for you he wouldn't be dead, so. No
apologies necessary.

JULIET
Yeah but like if you and I had just talked to each other we
wouldn't be like implicated in murder and stuff.

ROSALINE
Classic girl problems.

A pause.

WILLOW
Sooooo, like...

JULIET
There's a lake.

ROSALINE
Stones?

JULIET
Stones.

WILLOW
I saw a bucket for the horses near the entrance. For water.

ROSALINE
So we can wash away the blood.

JULIET

I have the vial.

WILLOW

We're gonna need to run. After we toss the body. I mean--

ROSALINE

Yeah the Prince is probably on his way and stuff. We should definitely run.

JULIET

Yeah, I mean, I'm already dead, so.

ROSALINE

I'm basically dead for how much attention anyone pays to me.

WILLOW

Yeah, being an indentured servant wasn't great either.

JULIET

I hear Venice is nice.

ROSALINE

Ooh, it's supposed to be pretty.

JULIET

And I don't mind wearing pants, I hear people are pretty easily fooled by pants and a ponytail under a hat.

> *They gather around Romeo's body and assume lifting positions.*

WILLOW

Are you two strong enough for this?

ROSALINE

Oh yeah.

JULIET

Yes. We are.

WILLOW

One.
Two.
Three--

Blackout as they're about to lift Romeo's body to go throw it in the lake.

AFTER HEREAFTER

Three WITCHES sit around a cave.

ELMGARD sits very still.

LENNY is eating popcorn.

VERITY paces.

In a corner, there is an anachronistic fax machine.

LENNY

Can you, like, stop that? It's annoying.

VERITY

(to herself)

I don't know how to stop it. I don't know how.

LENNY

Um, one foot stops, then the other foot stops.

VERITY

How can you make jokes right now?

ELMGARD

Indeed. This is no time for joking.

LENNY

You don't think any time / is for--

ELMGARD

/ No time is for joking. We fulfill our fated duties as the Weird Sisters, hand in hand--

LENNY AND VERITY

Posters of the sea and land,

LENNY

Fed Hecate's prophecies by the anachronistic fax machine in our drippy cold cave, we know.

VERITY

But people are DEAD.

Lenny eats more popcorn.

LENNY

It's kind of awesome.

ELMGARD

Our sacred duty is not "awesome" in the colloquial sense. It is awe-full, as in, full of awe, as in, mortals bow before our power.

VERITY

What power? I don't have any power! I didn't choose this!

ELMGARD

It is not our fate to choose.

LENNY

Which is why everything is so BORING. Which is why it's so exciting when they die.

VERITY

Oh my Hecate.

LENNY

Boring, boring, boring. We have this conversation every time. Verity gets high and mighty about morality, Elmgard gets stuck-up about our sacred duty, I get bored. This is just like every single other time something exciting has happened. And the last time something exciting happened

LENNY (continued)

was like FIVE ENTIRE CENTURIES AGO because most of
our sacred prophecies are about, like, who will inherit the
sheep farm. So like could we skip to the part where you shut
up and stop pacing so I can do mental replays of the gory
war-suicide-swordfight thing and enjoy my popcorn?

VERITY

I'm leaving.

LENNY

Great idea, go for a walk.

VERITY

I'm leaving the Weird Sisters.

A moment.

ELMGARD

As you are emotional, I will deign to forget you said that.

VERITY

Of course I'm emotional! Four thousand and twenty-six
people died, including at least nine murdered kids and one
totally preventable suicide, the kingdom is in shambles, and
we're sitting here like we had nothing to do with it!

LENNY

It's not like the kids wouldn't've died of typhoid.

ELMGARD

We are Hecate's agents of fate. We do not question our
prophecies or their aftereffects.

LENNY

Wish we did. It might be less BORING.

VERITY

We need to. I need to. I'm leaving.

LENNY

There's the door. ...The cave-opening.

VERITY

You should leave too.

ELMGARD

I will never abandon my post. And neither will you. Just because some mortals got a little enthusiastic with their pointy sticks--

VERITY

We told some psychopath that he would be king, and he and his partner in crime murdered practically everyone, and she went insane and killed herself, and he died in a swordfight but not until after a giant civil war, and now the kingdom is ruled by some blueblood with zero experience who has no idea how to handle shell-shocked Macduff and his dead-family trauma.

LENNY

Wow, you got all of that from overhearing those travelers?

VERITY

I'm making some inferences.

ELMGARD

Ours is not to make some inferences.

VERITY

Things are never going to be INTERESTING unless we make them interesting, Lenny. Come with me. Stop being a pawn in Hecate's twisted game.

26

ELMGARD

That is enough. Our goddess would be horrified to hear you talking like that.

VERITY

Well, she's not here, is she? The prophecies just come through the fax machine. She hasn't actually made an appearance in thousands of years. For all we know, she put that thing on auto-prophecy or ChatGPT and went to Aruba! We could be starting wars that kill all of these people for nothing!

LENNY

Aruba hasn't been established yet.

VERITY

Oh shut up, you know the space-time continuum thing gets confusing in here, go choke on your popcorn.

LENNY

You're right.

ELMGARD

Please do not attempt self-harm via popcorn.

LENNY

No, you're right, things will be interesting if we MAKE THEM INTERESTING.

ELMGARD

Oh, no.

LENNY

EVERY prophecy could be bloody and gory and terrible.

VERITY

Or we could stop making prophecies.

LENNY

Or we could make EXCITING ones.

ELMGARD

I think it is time for the Weird Sisters to have some quiet time.

LENNY

Why not just tell EVERYONE they're going to be king. More swordfights.

VERITY

No. No no no.

ELMGARD

Let us return to our normal post-prophecy routine of brewing potions, praying to Hecate, and growing sweet potatoes.

LENNY

Why have I been letting Elmgard set the tone?

VERITY

That is not the right question here.

LENNY

I don't even like sweet potatoes!

ELMGARD

They are a perfect vegetable!

LENNY

Not a vegetable!

VERITY

WE NEED TO MAKE THE WORLD BETTER, NOT
WORSE!

LENNY

Why?

VERITY

The space-time continuum dumped some dystopian young
adult novels in the back of the cave a few weeks ago and
I've been reading them during prayer time, and after this
massacre I have come to the realization that we are the
oppressors.

ELMGARD

You are meant to PRAY during prayer time!

LENNY

I'm never going to pray again.

ELMGARD

Oh Hecate, strike down those who do not obey you.

VERITY

We should be the change in the world we want to see!

LENNY

Sure, and I want bloodier storylines!

ELMGARD

HECATE. I BEG OF YOU.

LENNY

She's not listening.

ELMGARD

HECATE, IF YOUR GREAT EARS CAN DECIPHER A HINT OF THIS BLASPHEMY, I BEG OF YOU, STRIKE LENNY DOWN WHERE SHE STANDS.

A held moment.

They all wait to see if Hecate strikes Lenny down.

Nope.

Lenny starts laughing.

LENNY

I can do whatever I want.

ELMGARD

You are a Weird Sister. I am a Weird Sister. This is who we are.

LENNY

You just tried to get me struck down by your goddess.

ELMGARD

OUR goddess. Hecate is OUR goddess.

VERITY

Not anymore.

LENNY

Hey, space-time continuum! I demand better snacks! I'm sick of this random dumping-stuff-here-when-you-feel-like-it, especially when it's always popcorn! Brownie bites, please!

Also nothing.

LENNY

Okay, well, worth a try.

VERITY

Your greatest wish from the space-time continuum is really brownie bites?

LENNY

What's yours, world peace?

VERITY

MAYBE!

ELMGARD

Just because Hecate hasn't struck you down yet doesn't mean she won't.

VERITY

And that's your greatest wish in life? To do what you were told to do thousands of years ago?

ELMGARD

Oh, I'm sorry that being an agent of FATE HERSELF isn't good enough for the two of you!

VERITY

Again, maybe not fate! Maybe monkeys or AI!

LENNY

What if everything is random chaos and all we can do is amuse ourselves?

VERITY
We definitely shouldn't keep doing THIS!

Verity goes over to the fax machine and tries to wrench it away from the cave wall.

It's way too easy.

ELMGARD
You severed its magic.

VERITY
I didn't.

ELMGARD
You will be struck down where you stand!

VERITY
Sure, probably, but I'm saying, I didn't unplug it. It was already unplugged.

They look at Lenny.

Lenny tries to look innocent.

LENNY
It's a magical anachronistic fax machine that supposedly regurgitates prophecies from Hecate via the space-time continuum, it didn't need to be plugged in.

VERITY
But it was plugged in.

ELMGARD

It was plugged in. And no one is supposed to touch the magical anachronistic fax machine that brings forth prophecies from our eternal goddess Hecate via the space-time continuum--

VERITY

Lenny. Did you...

ELMGARD

Did you TOUCH the magical anachronistic fax machine that / brings forth prophecies--

VERITY

Did you make that king prophecy up?

LENNY
(lying badly)
What? No. I just had that idea, remember, Elmgard, inspired by Hecate's final prophecy. Which now that Verity has ruined the fax machine, is all we have to go on, so we should do more prophecies like that. "You will be king, go kill everyone," you know, that's clearly what Hecate wants us to do.

VERITY

You made that prophecy up. You unplugged the fax machine and you made that prophecy up!

ELMGARD
(to Lenny)
You were the one receiving the blessings of the prophecies that day...

VERITY

And Elmgard was farming sweet potatoes and I was reading
the Hunger Games and...

LENNY

Okay, so, what's the difference? If it was me, or ChatGPT?
This is more fun!

ELMGARD

Oh Hecate, oh triple-blessed triple-cursed goddess of all
existence and eternal nihilism, I beg of you...

VERITY AND LENNY

Strike Lenny down where she stands, we know.

VERITY

But she didn't. Strike you down.

LENNY

Exactly! So clearly it's fine!

ELMGARD

Oh wondrous most terrible goddess--

VERITY

Clearly it's fine.

ELMGARD

Oh awe-full being to whom I have dedicated the last
thousand years of my humble and unworthy life--

LENNY

She's not going to strike me down, get over it--

ELMGARD

I RENOUNCE YOU!!!

A moment.

VERITY

Elmgard, did you just... renounce... Hecate?

LENNY

Um.

ELMGARD

She has no power. She is not here. She did not strike you
down.

LENNY

Right.

ELMGARD

Although I asked THRICE.

VERITY

Right.

ELMGARD

Then I renounce her. Did you think me a fool, to believe in
that which has proven false?

LENNY

...yes?

VERITY

Thank you, Elmgard. Thank you. You are wise. You are so
wise! And now we can set the purpose of our existence to /
making the world a better place.

LENNY AND ELMGARD
/ Making our own bloody prophecies.

VERITY
No. NO!

LENNY
Elmgard... did you just agree with me?

ELMGARD
Why are you both so surprised that I can change my mind?

LENNY
Because you haven't changed it in thousands of--never
mind! Love you, sister! Let's get some mortals killed!

VERITY
You're siding with LENNY?

LENNY
I take offense to the tone of that comment.

ELMGARD
Verity... I have spent thousands of years worshipping at the
altar of one righteous goddess who failed me. I have no
interest in choosing another.

LENNY
Ooh, burn.

VERITY
So that's it, then. Give a mouse a cookie.

ELMGARD
What?

VERITY

Something the space-time continuum said.

ELMGARD

These mortals think they're so important. They think the
world revolves around them, and what fate wants for them.
We dedicated our immortal lives to handing down fate's
knowledge to them. I think it's time we get our revenge.

VERITY

But we just GOT our revenge! Or Lenny did! Lenny just got
so many of them killed with her fake prophecy!

ELMGARD

And it was awesome.

ELMGARD and LENNY high-five.

VERITY

I guess I'm leaving.

LENNY

Take the popcorn. You'll get hungry.

VERITY

I'll prophesy against you. I'll prophesy good things.

LENNY

And what will you do when they don't happen?

ELMGARD

That's bleak. And so true.

LENNY

I like New Elmgard.

They high five again.

VERITY

I'll rely on humans' better instincts. I'll convince them to be loyal, and good, and trust each other--

LENNY

And get murdered?

VERITY

There HAS to be a way for them to be good.

ELMGARD

Why?

VERITY

I can't believe my sisters are both psychopaths.

ELMGARD

No, I ask you, Verity. Why do you believe mortals can be good? You know why I like hanging out with my sweet potatoes? Because they don't shout at me and throw stones. They don't curse me and poke at me with pitchforks because I have a couple of warts. Sweet potatoes don't tell me that we can coexist and then push me back, and back, and back, until my sisters and I live in a drippy cave with an anachronistic fax machine. They don't hate me.

LENNY

They don't come to me for help with their sick baby and then blame me when the baby dies. They don't promise me love, and kindness, and loyalty, they don't tell me we can be friends, that we can be more than friends, and then decide when their baby dies that I was cursed all along and they must harden their heart against me. They don't send search parties of guards out into Birnam Wood to look for the

LENNY (continued)

murderer of their child, to try to kill me, even when all I did was help, even when all I did was help and fall in love.

VERITY

Lady Macbeth?

LENNY

She said she loved me, would love me forever if I could only save her baby. But there was nothing I could do.

ELMGARD

Oh, Lenny.

VERITY

Oh, Lenny.

LENNY

Some people deserve bloody prophecies.

ELMGARD

Yes. They all do.

VERITY

Elmgard--

ELMGARD

Listen. They all deserve bloody prophecies. Prophecies, not realities. We didn't kill anyone. Lenny didn't kill anyone. No one put that knife in Macbeth's hand, except maybe Lady Macbeth, but no one made him do it. No one made them go insane with greed and ambition. All we did was say he would be king. And look what he did with it. You want the best of humankind, Verity? Telling them "good things" won't make that happen. Give them the worst prophecy, and see who can ignore it. Give them the chance to be good.

LENNY

And when it goes bad, we can watch and laugh.

ELMGARD

And if it goes bad, we can eat popcorn together.

Verity hesitates.

LENNY

You're not the oppressor, Verity. None of us are. If we find a human who will ignore my bloody prophecies, I'll be happier than you. If we find a human who will ignore my bloody prophecies, I'll be the first to give up my prophecy game and go live in the land of mortals again. Because it'll mean we can. That they are strong enough to be good, and true enough to mean it when they say they won't hurt us, wise enough to not pick up pitchforks when they see our faces. But until that day, I'll be here, testing them. Seeing if it's safe for us.

ELMGARD

(to Verity)
What do you think? ...Sister?

LENNY

(to Verity)
Please stay. It's not safe out there. Not yet.

VERITY

You really think it might be? One day?

ELMGARD

One day.

LENNY

One day.

They join hands.

ELMGARD, LENNY, AND VERITY
The weird sisters, hand in hand, posters of the sea and land--

> *Something is tossed onstage next to them,*
> *summoned by their unity.*

> *It's a package of brownie bites.*

VERITY
Brownie bites.

IAGO'S DAUGHTER

A teenage girl, ABBY, is doing laundry by hand. A second teenage girl, BRITTANY, enters, and immediately checks all sides of the space for exits, holds up a cloak from the laundry basket to see if it might fit her, etc. ABBY ignores her for a moment. Then:

ABBY
Are you gonna help do the laundry or just keep plotting your escape?

BRITTANY
Oh hi! I'm Brittany. Short for Brittanica. But I'd prefer to be just Brittany, no backstory, thank you very much.

ABBY
Okay, so, you gonna help with the laundry, or...?

BRITTANY
You gonna tell on me?

ABBY
Depends if you get on my nerves.

BRITTANY
Is there a back door to this place?

Abby just stares at her, then rolls her eyes.

Brittany picks up some laundry and starts washing it. Except she's never done laundry before in her life, and it shows.

ABBY
Well, you've definitely never done laundry before.

43

BRITTANY

Rude.

ABBY

Never done a chore, already plotting escape... Noble's
daughter, for sure. Useless.

BRITTANY

Why are you so rude??

ABBY

Sorry your family didn't approve of your starcrossed love or
whatever and banished you here. "Oh no. I have to do
laundry with a peasant."

BRITTANY

What about you? So awful your parents sent you away?

ABBY

My parents are dead.

BRITTANY

...Sorry.

ABBY

They weren't great people.

BRITTANY

Still, sorry.

Abby says nothing and continues to do laundry.

BRITTANY

Mine are alive, they're just super freaked out about me ever
marrying anyone in case my husband gets hypnotized by his
standard-bearer and strangles me.

ABBY

That's... very specific.

BRITTANY

Yeah. This whole country has Desdemona fever. You don't know the half of it.

ABBY

I think I do.

BRITTANY

Trust me. It's worse when you're her cousin. --Do you think they'd notice if I take this?

Brittany holds up another cloak to see if it'll fit her.

Abby laughs.

ABBY

Really?

BRITTANY

I don't think it's that funny actually? I'm trying to figure out a way out of here?

ABBY

They really sent Desdemona's cousin to... oh wow... they really sent Desdemona's cousin--

BRITTANY

I'm actually sick of being called that, my name is Brittany--

ABBY

They actually sent Desdemona's cousin to do laundry with Iago's daughter.

Brittany stops trying to figure out escape-cloak sizing.

BRITTANY

That's not funny.

ABBY

No, it REALLY is.

BRITTANY

Just because my stupid cousin married a stupid guy who went full domestic violence because of some stupid RUMOR started by a stupid jealous PEASANT everyone thinks they get to make jokes and pretend they're related to Iago or Othello or something. It's not actually funny. My cousin actually died. And my parents are so scared I'll somehow die too that they sent me to this NUNNERY to do the nuns' LAUNDRY while I make up my mind if I want to be a BRIDE OF GOD and you're apparently going to tell on me if I try to CHECK FOR EXITS so my life sucks enough so if you could just not laugh thanks ever so much, I can mess up this menial task in SILENCE while I subtly plot my escape.

ABBY

Boo-hoo, your life sounds SO horrible.

BRITTANY

Shut UP.

ABBY

Try being Iago's daughter. Seriously. And before you ask, no, I'm not a mass murderer, I don't plan on conducting any nefarious plots to get you strangled, and my dad wasn't that nice to me either, he literally murdered my mother.

BRITTANY

You're...

ABBY

Abby. Abigaille. Actually Iago's daughter. Would prefer to be known as Emilia's daughter even though she also wasn't the greatest mom. Yes.

Abby sighs and moves as far from Brittany as possible.

BRITTANY

What are you doing?

ABBY

Giving you some space so the rocks hurt less when they hit me.

BRITTANY

I don't have any rocks.

ABBY

You'll find something. They all do.

BRITTANY

People... throw rocks at you?

ABBY

Go ahead. Run away for all I care. Just don't hit my face.

BRITTANY

Sorry.

ABBY

For what.

BRITTANY

Sorry that people are mean to you because of your dad.
That's rude.

ABBY

Right. Um. ...Sorry that people are mean to you because your
cousin died.

BRITTANY

People are the worst.

ABBY

Yeah.

> *Abby looks at Brittany's laundry, starts to go*
> *over, then stops, looks at the laundry again.*

BRITTANY

Are you... okay?

ABBY

You swear you're not pretending to be cool so I'll get closer
and you can try to strangle me?

BRITTANY

That's... no. I mean, yes, I swear.

ABBY

You're sure.

BRITTANY

I solemnly promise not to throw rocks at you, try to strangle
you, or otherwise cause you bodily harm.

ABBY

Good, cause you're really not scrubbing that, like, at all. And before you make your Grand Escape or whatever, you should probably pretend a little better or Mother Superior will notice.

Abby goes to Brittany, takes the laundry from her, and shows her how to do it right.

BRITTANY

Oh.

ABBY

Yeah. It's actually hard.

BRITTANY

Then why are you doing it?

ABBY

What do you mean?

BRITTANY

Um, hello, we've already been sent to a nunnery in the middle of nowhere and aren't even eligible to be nuns yet, so like, what else are they going to do to us? Why are you actually doing the chores?

ABBY

Okay, Milady Brittany.

BRITTANY

Shut up.

ABBY

Some of us have been doing chores forever.

BRITTANY

Okay, but like, if your parents are dead then like--wait. Is
your dad actually dead?

ABBY

Dead, being tortured eternally in some prison, whatever.
Dead to me, for sure.

BRITTANY

Right. Yeah. So like who is actually in CHARGE of you?

ABBY

Mother Superior?

BRITTANY

Mother Superior who literally doesn't care about us, only
cares about the laundry getting done?

ABBY

Yeah? Are you just trying to make me feel worse?

BRITTANY

No. I'm like, fomenting revolution.

ABBY

Okay...?

BRITTANY

Put down the laundry.

ABBY

No.

BRITTANY

Put down the laundry!

ABBY

NO!

BRITTANY

Why are you acting like Iago's daughter?

ABBY

Excuse me, what?

BRITTANY

You're just here and you're gonna, like, be grumpy and suffer forever because of your murder-y dad?

ABBY

I guess so, thanks!

BRITTANY

Nope.

ABBY

Oh wow, you've fixed my entire life by saying nope. Guess I'll never do a chore again.

She keeps scrubbing.

BRITTANY

Abby! You don't deserve to suffer!

ABBY

Yeah, thanks, but I'm gonna.

BRITTANY

No. You really don't deserve to suffer. And neither do I.

ABBY

Okay, laundry is NOT a fate worse than death, noblegirl--

BRITTANY

Come with me.

ABBY

WHAT?

BRITTANY

You and me. Let's escape.

ABBY

If you're just trying to get me to tell you where the back door is, it doesn't take a genius, it's in the back.

BRITTANY

No, I mean it. Come with me.

ABBY

Yeah, I can see why your parents sent you to a nunnery for safekeeping, cause you're not living in the real world. "Escape" is not a thing.

BRITTANY

We could go to--what happened to your parents' house?

ABBY

Their hut? Got burned down. Is now a memorial to Desdemona's memory.

BRITTANY

Oh. Okay, well, what about relatives?

ABBY

Their huts got burned down too. People went pretty
scorched-earth on the family.

BRITTANY

What about...

ABBY

I don't have any OPTIONS, noblegirl. Some of us don't
come from silk cushions and the luxury of marrying well.
Some of us were born to do laundry. And doing it
somewhere I won't get stoned to death because of my dad is
probably the safest plan.

BRITTANY

But... you're just going to live here forever?

ABBY

Um... yeah. And so are you, 'cause they don't just let noble
daughters walk out the back door.

BRITTANY

No. No no no. I'm not letting you accept this. I'm not just
ACCEPTING this.

ABBY

Why not? It's better than marriage. You could get someone
who strangles you. Or someone who conspires to get
someone else strangled.

BRITTANY

That's rude.

ABBY

Okay, but--

BRITTANY

I thought we agreed not to throw our families in each other's faces.

ABBY

I'm just telling the truth.

BRITTANY

Like, my cousin is actually DEAD, and maybe I didn't like her that much because all she talked about was all the battles her husband was in, but like STILL, we were RELATED, and I don't appreciate all the strangling talk, okay?

ABBY

Yeah, and my mom got stabbed for telling the truth, so I don't appreciate the "everything's just gonna work out if I do the right thing for me and my girls" attitude, okay?

BRITTANY

Ooh, am I your girl?

ABBY

THAT's what you took away from that?

BRITTANY

I've never really had a friend before. Just maids and Desdemona.

ABBY

Okay, there's a lot to unpack there, but--

BRITTANY

I have horses!

ABBY

Wow.

BRITTANY

I have horses, their names are Middleton and Staffordshire, I was going through an Anglo-Saxon phase, okay--

ABBY

Uh-huh--

BRITTANY

And I can get them for us and we can ride to, to--

ABBY

To...?

BRITTANY

Off into the sunset! We can figure that part out later!

ABBY

Brittany.

BRITTANY

I have a widowed aunt in Ravenna. I think she's probably old enough that she would love the company and wouldn't ask too many questions.

ABBY

Ravenna??

BRITTANY

Okay, yeah. Horses, Ravenna, widowed aunt.

ABBY

And, what, then I do YOUR laundry forever?

BRITTANY

What? No. My aunt has staff for that.

ABBY

Child...

BRITTANY

Sorry. Is "staff" offensive? I've literally never had a friend before.

ABBY

You seriously want to be my "friend"? ...So you're gonna raise me up to nobility and we'll live with your widowed aunt and have flings with passing lords, is that the plan?

BRITTANY

Honestly, yeah. Sounds great, right?

ABBY

And when your parents get word you're gone?

BRITTANY

I'll send them a letter from Aunt Mabel's.

ABBY

And when they show up to Aunt Mabel's to collect you?

BRITTANY

Why are you being such a killjoy?

ABBY

Do you know why my mom stayed with my dad all those years?

BRITTANY

Umm... because she misguidedly loved him with a passion he didn't deserve?

                    ABBY

Absolutely not.

                  BRITTANY

Because he had great hair?

                    ABBY

You're getting colder.

                  BRITTANY

I really don't know any positive qualities of the guy who
killed my cousin and your mom.

                    ABBY

He didn't have any. My mom didn't stay with him because
she loved him, or he had great anything, or he had any
redeeming qualities whatsoever. She stayed with him
because the only thing more dangerous than being stuck
under one roof with a violent man... is not having a roof at
all.

                  BRITTANY

But we would, like, have a roof.

                    ABBY

At your widowed aunt's. Who won't tell your parents and
who will definitely be cool with me lounging about. Whose
house you can definitely navigate to from here.

                  BRITTANY

We could figure it out!

ABBY

Or we could not! Seriously, Brittany! Do you not understand
what could happen to us out there on the road?

BRITTANY

Better than the NOTHING that will happen to us here!

ABBY

NO! It isn't.

BRITTANY

Oh, sorry, wait, are you called to be a bride of God? Because
I didn't mean to be like, offensive, or whatever, that's
obviously a really cool thing to do, I'm just not actually
called to it--

ABBY

I don't get to be a bride of God, Brittany, it doesn't matter if
I'm called to it or not, I'm not here temporarily like you
while you figure out your calling. I'm lowborn. My choices
are kitchen or laundry, wait actually the kitchen's full, my
choice is laundry or laundry.

BRITTANY

And you don't want to run away.

ABBY

I don't think you're following. Road. Bad things. Servitude.
Worse. Men like my dad and your cousin's husband.

BRITTANY

Right but...

ABBY

This is the best possible place we could be.

BRITTANY

HERE?

ABBY

No men. No parents controlling us. I get my chores done, I get to do whatever I want, because no one cares where I go or what I do. You do your prayers, you get to write the next great Italian novel in your spare time. You really think you were gonna find a husband who'd let you do that?

BRITTANY

How did you know I'm an author?

ABBY

The imagination. Definitely not that every literate noble wants to write a novel. Look, Brittany, I know you want to make a splash and have an adventure, but sometimes, you're already in the best possible world.

BRITTANY

That's sad.

ABBY

No. It's not. I'm not staying here because I have to, Brittany. I'm staying here because I've considered all the options, I've thought about what marriage would be, what traveling would mean, what running away would bring, what becoming a thief would bring. And I've realized... out there, I'm either Iago or Emilia. But in here... I can just be Abby. I don't mind doing a little laundry, to get to have my own little space in this world. And maybe to have a friend or whatever. Especially if we split the chores, we can have so much time. We can be ourselves. So you can go if you want to. You can try to find your horse Staffordshire and gallop to Ravenna and probably do more chores in your widowed aunt's house than you'd have to here. You can go and try really, really

ABBY (continued)

hard to be okay, try really, really hard to make a safe corner for yourself. Or you could stay here, and not have to worry about any of that. You could stay here, and hang out with someone who isn't just Iago's daughter, who doesn't see you as just Desdemona's cousin. You could stay here, and be my friend.

> *Brittany looks at Abby for a moment. Then she exits.*
>
> *Abby sighs and goes back to scrubbing laundry. Brittany comes back in, wrapping cloth around her hands to protect them from the laundry scrapers.*
>
> *They look at each other.*
> *Brittany sits down and starts scrubbing for real.*

THE REVENGE OF GERTRUDE

*The throne room, Denmark. The bodies of
Hamlet, Laertes, Claudius, and Gertrude lie on
the ground. Osric, Horatio, Ambassador, and
assorted Courtiers watch in dismay as
Fortinbras claims the throne.*

FORTINBRAS
Let four captains
Bear Hamlet like a soldier to the stage;

*He waits for someone to do this. Osric, Horatio,
and Ambassador struggle to lift Hamlet's body
up to the dais. It's hard and they probably slip.*

FORTINBRAS
For he was likely, had he been put on,
To have prov'd most royally; and for his passage
The soldiers' music and the rites of war
Speak loudly for him.
Take up the bodies. Such a sight as this
Becomes the field but here shows much amiss.
Go, bid the soldiers shoot.

Gertrude sits up, looks around.

GERTRUDE
Oh hush, you carbuncle.

Everyone screams.

FORTINBRAS
A GHOST! THE GHOST OF THE QUEEN!

OSRIC
Er--Queen Gertrude?

FORTINBRAS

She was dead. You all saw she was dead, right? Like,
Horatio just totally said she died. Just now. Which means
I'm king now. And she's a DEMON GHOST!

GERTRUDE

You have to actually die to be a ghost, Fortinbras. I took a
fake nap.

AMBASSADOR

I knew I should never have taken a job at court.

Hamlet sits up.

Everyone screams.

HORATIO

HAMLET???? Hamlet, you're alive! This is the best day
ever!

HAMLET

Oh, woe is me, I have arrived in hell.

GERTRUDE

Of all the sodden-witted knaves. You're alive, you stupid
boy.

COURTIERS

THE PRINCE LIVES!!!

GERTRUDE

Wow, way to care when I woke up. But yeah.

FORTINBRAS

No. I'm king. I'm the king of Denmark!!

OSRIC

I'm so sorry, sir, but I don't think you are. Because the Queen and the Prince are still alive, so--

Laertes sits up.

Everyone screams. Then sees it's Laertes and doesn't really care anymore.

COURTIER 1

Oh, it's just him.

FORTINBRAS

Who the heck is that, another prince?? I came all the way from NORWAY for this and now they're all bloody alive?

OSRIC

Oh no, that's just Laertes. Not royal or anything.

FORTINBRAS

Okay, great. King king king!

LAERTES

Oh, fortunate I am, that I am in hell! Now I may see my wonderful sister Ophelia!

HORATIO

This isn't hell. For you, anyway. I am so confused.

HAMLET

Oh woe is me, that I tread this earth another sorrowed while.

LAERTES

No Ophelia?

GERTRUDE

Can everyone please SHUT UP?

Everyone shuts up and looks at Gertrude.

GERTRUDE

THANK you. Now, I feel like it's fairly obvious what
happened here if you think about it for literally one second...

*Waits for them to get it. Everyone just stares at
her blankly. Fortinbras has an idea.*

FORTINBRAS

I'm king!

GERTRUDE

No. I replaced the poison with honey.

LAERTES

Honey??

GERTRUDE

You didn't really think you and my ex were being QUIET,
did you? With your grand plan to poison my son, poison the
rapiers, poison the drink? All the shhhh, shhhh, no one can
hear, we shall poison Hamlet, we're being such great spies,
three-inch fools.

OSRIC

Um, your majesty? By your ex do you mean--

GERTRUDE

Claudius. I refuse to call him husband. And thankfully he's
really dead. Hamlet, like, stabbed him in the stomach
because he thought the poison thing was real. And then he
made him chug honey, but like, stomach wounds are a lot

GERTRUDE (continued)

more fatal than honey.

Pause for literally no one to mourn Claudius.

OSRIC

I feel like someone should say something here for the king, but like...

COURTIER 1

He really sucked. I mean.

HAMLET

Dastardly wicked creature, I rejoice on your grave!

GERTRUDE

Mm-hmm, yeah. So like I was saying--

FORTINBRAS

Hamlet killed the king so he's a traitor so he goes to jail and I'm king!

GERTRUDE

Honestly. Can someone--

AMBASSADOR

I got it.

Ambassador escorts Fortinbras offstage.

AMBASSADOR

Let's go get you a nice drinkie, all right?

FORTINBRAS

But I came all the way from NORWAY.

AMBASSADOR
I know, I know, it's not fair. It's not fair at ALL.

FORTINBRAS
I recited the WHOLE SPEECH even though I don't know some of those words.

AMBASSADOR
You did GREAT. Really, you knocked it out of the park.

FORTINBRAS
Knocked what?

AMBASSADOR
Never mind. Hush now. Let's get you a drinkie and a treat.

And they're gone.

HAMLET
So I'm king now?

GERTRUDE
Oh s'blood I'm so tired. No.

LAERTES
Am I king?

HORATIO
How the bull's-pizzle would YOU be king?

LAERTES
You know, the rebellion thing, crowds of Danes calling for me to take the throne--

OSRIC

Right, that happened.

COURTIER 1

Honestly only because we were all sick of Claudius.

HAMLET

But if I'm not king...

LAERTES

And I'm not king...

HORATIO

Again, that was never going to happen...

OSRIC

Who's king???

They all look at each other.

Osric almost steps forward to claim the throne.

GERTRUDE

Oh, I am tempted. I am so tempted to wash my hands of all of you. I am so tempted to go drown in the brook...

LAERTES

Whoa whoa whoa.

HAMLET

MOM, you can't just SAY that after Ophelia--

LAERTES

Yeah, like, that's my SISTER who DROWNED, like--

GERTRUDE

OPHELIA IS NOT DEAD, SHE WENT TO START A NEW
LIFE IN VENICE AS A FLORIST. Come on, guys. You
really bought the whole "she drowned in a brook" thing?
Brooks aren't even DEEP. That brook comes up to like, your
ANKLES.

COURTIER 1

Ohhhhhh.

OSRIC

Oh wow.

COURTIER 2

GERTRUDE is King.

GERTRUDE

Unfortunately, yeah. I'm taking control of Denmark.
Because none of you lily-livered scoundrels can handle it.

HAMLET

Oh good.

LAERTES

Honestly, all yours.

HORATIO

Um, Hamlet, I thought you WANTED to be king.

HAMLET

God no. Let Mom do it. She's better. Except the whole
marrying-Claudius thing.

GERTRUDE

He literally had a dagger to my throat, you stock-fish.

HAMLET

WHAT?

GERTRUDE

Yeah, and when you confronted me in my chambers about how TERRIBLE I was and made me APOLOGIZE, you had a rapier. Did it really not occur to you that it's hard to tell the truth and stand up for yourself when a man has a SHARP WEAPON pointed at you??

LAERTES

Oh wow.

HAMLET

That... yeah. That really sucks, Mom, I'm sorry.

OSRIC

I'd just like to say that we should all do a better job of respecting women.

COURTIER 1

No one tell Fortinbras the sharp weapon thing works, he'll be back in here with a broadsword to threaten you. But we'll defend you with our lives!!

GERTRUDE

No need. After the whole dagger and then rapier thing I totally took some self-defense classes.

She picks up one of the rapiers.

GERTRUDE

En garde!   •

Everyone squeaks a little in fear.

GERTRUDE

Oh, and bandage your brainsickly arms, boys. Stop bleeding
all over my court.

HAMLET

Right.

LAERTES

Yes, ma'am.

OSRIC

I can't believe we never thought of Gertrude becoming king.

COURTIER 1

Yeah, she's doing like a great job.

COURTIER 2

Totally wild.

GERTRUDE

Great. Problem solved. A toast to our success.

> *Gertrude snaps her fingers and Courtier 3 pours
> everyone some champagne or whatever.*

OSRIC

To the reign of Gertrude!

ALL

The reign of Gertrude!

> *They drink.*

GERTRUDE

Great. Now let's all go take a nap.

There is a loud knock at the court doors.

HORATIO

Who's that?

GERTRUDE

If that's Fortinbras again, I swear on all that is holy--

> *The doors crash down. OPHELIA and an*
> *ensemble of WARRIOR MAIDSERVANTS storm*
> *in, armed.*

LAERTES

Sister!

HAMLET

My love!

OPHELIA

Shut up.

HAMLET

But I love you. I was just pretending to be crazy. I really
really love you. So many lots.

> *Ophelia points her sword at Hamlet.*

OPHELIA

My name is Ophelia Poloniusdottir. You killed my father.
Prepare to die.

HAMLET

HA HA HA--

LAERTES

Ophelia, we like, figured all that out. Bygones bygones. We all tried to kill each other and stuff and went to hell but not hell and then anyway we kind of forgot about the dad dying thing, so can you like--

GERTRUDE AND OPHELIA

Silence!

OPHELIA

Don't "silence" my brother.

GERTRUDE

Don't "silence" my subject.

OPHELIA

Whatever. (to Hamlet) I challenge you to a duel to the death.

HAMLET

Um. Uh. Um. Baby?

GERTRUDE

I swear I raised you better than this.

HAMLET

Let's figure this out, baby. Let's talk it through. Maybe with a few fewer... clothes on? Yeah... let's "duel." Cue puns about "nothing" and "ladies' laps."

> *Ophelia growls and raises her sword in Hamlet's direction.*
>
> *But Hamlet starts to choke. Dramatically-- because Hamlet does everything dramatically-- he falls over.*

HAMLET

I am poison'd--poison'd! The drink! My dear throat that allows me to spout such fabulously dramatic words--it closeth--

He slumps. Is he dead??

HORATIO

My lord! My--lord--

Horatio starts to choke and fall too.

Then suddenly everyone who drank Gertrude's champagne--everyone except Ophelia, Gertrude, and Ophelia's warrior maidservants--is choking and foaming at the mouth and falling.

GERTRUDE

Like I said. Let's all take a nap.

Ophelia stares at Gertrude.

OPHELIA

What... the... you killed my BROTHER???

Ophelia charges Gertrude. Gertrude snatches up a rapier and parries. Warrior maidservants cheer.

WARRIOR MAIDSERVANTS

OPHELIA! OPHELIA!

They continue cheering throughout, generally causing mayhem.

GERTRUDE

Not really--

OPHELIA

I will END YOU!

GERTRUDE

Did you even--

Slash, parry--

GERTRUDE

LIKE your brother that much??

OPHELIA

You can't just kill people's BROTHERS! And your--

Slash, parry--

OPHELIA

You killed your own SON? That's cold!

GERTRUDE

You were about to--

Trip, slash--

GERTRUDE

MURDER him!

OPHELIA

Yeah, 'cause I'm not his MOM!

GERTRUDE

Did anyone ever tell HIM that?

Battle, battle, battle--

OPHELIA
I AM OPHELIA POLONIUSDOTTIR. YOU KILLED MY
BROTHER. PREPARE TO--

GERTRUDE
NO I DIDN'T.

OPHELIA
I literally just--

Slash, slash--

OPHELIA
Saw you kill him!

GERTRUDE
HE'S JUST ASLEEP!

*Ophelia pauses. WARRIOR MAIDSERVANTS
stop chanting. Warrior Maidservant 1 didn't get
the memo.*

WARRIOR MAIDSERVANT 1
Ophelia! Ophelia!

OPHELIA
Shut up, I want to hear this.

WARRIOR MAIDSERVANT 1
Sorry.

OPHELIA
Come again with ASLEEP?

GERTRUDE

Aren't you just sick of men?

OPHELIA

Yeah?

GERTRUDE

I knew it. I just knew it. They'd all be like, who's king?
Who's king? I'm king. Me! Even flipping Osric. So I
planned ahead.

OPHELIA

Skip to the part where my brother isn't dead.

GERTRUDE

I gave them all a sleeping potion so they can cool off in the
dungeons for a bit to adjust to bending to my rule.

OPHELIA

Oh.

GERTRUDE

Yeah?

OPHELIA

Really?

GERTRUDE

Really. You can check that they're breathing.

Ophelia checks. They are.

OPHELIA

...Okay, fair.

GERTRUDE

Right?

OPHELIA

Then why in the rotten apples did you swordfight me?

GERTRUDE

I mean, it's not like your maidservants were letting me talk--

OPHELIA

And?

GERTRUDE

And I really wanted to try out my new sword skills, okay?
And you know none of these idiots were gonna be bold
enough to come at me with a sword. They were just gonna
poison me behind my back like my first husband, RIP except
rot in hell.

OPHELIA

Right. The dungeon cool-off period is a good idea.

GERTRUDE

So... you're not gonna be a florist in Venice, huh?

OPHELIA

I can't believe you bought that story.

GERTRUDE

I knew you were lying, I just thought maybe you went to
become a pirate or something.

OPHELIA

Honestly, still on the table.

GERTRUDE
You're great with a sword.

OPHELIA
You too, tbh.

GERTRUDE
You'd be an awesome pirate.

OPHELIA
Aw thanks. Yeah, I'm considering it. I'm actually a really strong swimmer. Just picture it... the sea wind in my hair, going wherever I want on my well-decorated ship, murdering bros left and right...

GERTRUDE
I'd be an awesome pirate too.

OPHELIA
I mean, yeah.

GERTRUDE
Maybe...
She looks around at all the sleeping men.

OPHELIA
Are you thinking what I'm thinking?

GERTRUDE
Are YOU thinking what I'm thinking?

OPHELIA
(to maidservants)
Are you all thinking what we're thinking?

Gertrude goes to a chest behind the throne and

takes out a bunch of gold or jewelry or whatever.

GERTRUDE

Start-up financing?

OPHELIA

Start-up weapons.

She snaps her fingers and her warrior maidservants take whatever they want off of all the men's bodies. Weapons, gold, etc.

GERTRUDE

Ooh, Claudius has--

She grabs a gold chain off his bloody body, hands it to a warrior.

OPHELIA

You know I'll be taking a sabbatical to come back and fight Hamlet to the death, right?

GERTRUDE

Honestly, that's fair. In the meantime... let's pirate.

WARRIOR MAIDSERVANT 1

But what about your kingdom?

Gertrude looks around at all the men on the ground.

GERTRUDE

They deserve each other.

And Ophelia, Gertrude, and the warriors exit to become pirates.

OPTIONAL ENDING

Darkness. Then spooky music rises.

VERITY, LENNY, and ELMGARD stand over the fax machine, chanting.

VERITY, LENNY, AND ELMGARD
The weird sisters, hand in hand,
posters of the sea and land,
thus do go about, about,

Lenny does a not-spooky dance move.

LENNY
And as we do we shake it out--

VERITY
Thrice or however we actually want--

ELMGARD
Because we decide who fate will haunt!

LENNY
I imagine a world where captive queens

ELMGARD
Become pirates who will rule the seas

VERITY
And daughters who were once afraid

LENNY
Find friends and safety, and they stay.

ELMGARD

I imagine a world where young women don't die

VERITY

Where instead they live, adventure, and thrive--

LENNY

I imagine a world

VERITY, LENNY, AND ELMGARD

Where witches rise,
with joy, with moons, with ocean tides...

*And they blow onto the fax machine, and
darkness descends, and we hear the sound of a
fax printing...*

*Which segues into the sound of ocean waves...
Against a boat?*

*Lights up on a swaying Willow, Rosaline, and
Juliet, looking seasick.*

JULIET

Oh 'sblood 'sblood 'sblood I'm gonna be sick--

WILLOW

I TOLD you you should've drank some of my herbs--

JULIET

Shut up--

ROSALINE

Honestly, Juliet, just because you like stabbed your husband
dead-y dead you think you're stronger than the ocean?
Waves literally do not care how brave you are.

                    WILLOW
You're turning green.

                    JULIET
Can I please have some herbs?

                    WILLOW
Oh I totally took them all a while ago.

                    ROSALINE
Um hey--

                    JULIET
You took ALL of them?

                    ROSALINE
Hey gals--

                    WILLOW
You said you didn't WANT any--

                    JULIET
Rude.

                    ROSALINE
HEY SHUT UP!

            *A crash and the hooting and hollering of a band
            of warrior maidens, led by Ophelia and
            Gertrude.*

                    JULIET
WHAT WAS THAT?

ROSALINE

I think our ship to Venice just got boarded.

*Ophelia, Gertrude, and the warrior maidens
storm on, pirates, armed to the teeth.*

OPHELIA

Yeah, you did. Your money or your lives.

WILLOW

Oh 'sblood.

ROSALINE

Of course. The second I try to make a NEW LIFE for myself
or whatever--

JULIET

Are you PIRATES?

GERTRUDE

You heard Ophelia. Money...

ROSALINE

I just try to get to Venice to finally chill outside the court
away from stupid men and--

WILLOW

Ros--

ROSALINE

Of COURSE there are flipping PIRATES in the way--

JULIET

We don't have any money. We, um, murdered my husband in
a tomb and tossed his body in a lake and snuck onto this boat
as stowaways in pants?

WILLOW
Are you INSANE? Don't CONFESS!

OPHELIA
Hmmm.

GERTRUDE
Hmmm.

They confer quietly for a second. Then more loudly:

OPHELIA
YOU have to teach them how to swordfight.

GERTRUDE
Ugh. They're children.

OPHELIA
But you're the one with the better backhand slide.

GERTRUDE
(blushing)
Oh my gosh, stop.

JULIET
So are you gonna, like, kill us, or...?

OPHELIA
You wanna go pretend to be dudes in Venice, or bring your murder skills aboard?

WILLOW
Join PIRATES?

ROSALINE
Is ANYTHING far-fetched at this point?

WILLOW
No, just like, oh my gosh, this is the best day of my life.

JULIET
Up to you, Ros. I know you wanted Venice.

ROSALINE
You're letting ME decide?

JULIET
About time you got to.

GERTRUDE
Ahem. Can we get a decision here?

> *With ceremony, Rosaline bows to Ophelia and Gertrude.*

ROSALINE
We would be honored.

> *Without ceremony, Ophelia, Gertrude, and the warrior maidens toss Rosaline, Juliet, and Willow some swords.*

OPHELIA
Great, cause the crew's coming this way. Let's take this boat.

> *As one, they all raise their swords and charge offstage.*